PEOPLES OF THE MARITIMES

The Micmac

Stephen A. Davis

For years, English-speaking people used the spelling Micmac.
We've moved to Mi'kmaq, the spelling preferred by the Mi'kmaq,
using their own orthography. Because the interior text pages of this
book were first printed in 1991, they retain the spelling as Micmac.

Nimbus Publishing Limited
PO Box 9301, Station A
Halifax, NS B3K 5N5
(902) 455-4286

Editor: Douglas Beall
Design: Paul McCormick
Cover photo: Harold McGee
Printed and bound in Canada

Canadian Cataloguing in Publication Data

Davis, Stephen A., 1949—
Micmac
(Peoples of the Maritimes)
Originally published: Tantallon, N.S.: Four East Publications, 1991.
Includes bibliographical references.
ISBN 1-55109-180-1
1. Micmac Indians—History. I. Title. II. Series.
E99.M6D38 1996   971.5'004973   C96-950112-9

The peoples of the Maritimes comprise in excess of seventy distinct and identifiable ethnic-cultural groups. Yet, only a few of these have their place in our history and our society well known and documented. The Peoples of the Maritimes series is an attempt to redress that imbalance by providing a well researched but readable collection of monographs for both the general and student reader.

The demographic face of Canada as a whole is changing rapidly as a result of national realities connected with the country's declining birth rate and the need for more immigrants to enhance economic growth. In this context, education and information are crucial for the promotion of harmonious social change.

The Maritimes has a rich diversity in its population, ranging all the way from the first nations and the pre-Confederation settlers to the later nation builders from all parts of the globe—more recently from Third World countries in increasing numbers. The literature on the Maritimes must keep pace with these changing times and challenges.

The Maritimes Peoples Project gratefully acknowledges the funding assistance provided for the development of this book by the Minister responsible for Multiculturalism, Government of Canada.

Bridglal Pachai, Ph.D.
General Editor

The author is grateful for research assistance given by Ms. Sherry Pictou who, although pursuing full-time studies, provided her valuable time and insight into contemporary Micmac culture. The original artwork for this book was done by Ms. Teresa MacPhee, an accomplished Micmac artist studying at the Nova Scotia College of Art and Design. Her vivid images and sensitivity to Micmac culture will insure that future generations will share in Micmac experience. Additional research and many of the illustrations found throughout this book were done with the able assistance of Mr. Laird Niven. The original manuscript was word processed by Ms. Monica Lewis.

The author would like to extend his kindest appreciation to all of the Micmac who generously provided their time and interest to this book. Unfortunately, a general work such as this is limited and cannot represent the total history of accomplishments of the Native peoples of the Maritimes. The author accepts complete responsibility for errors of omission, with the hope that what does appear represents a small contribution to an understanding of the Micmac.

Stephen A. Davis
Halifax, June 1991

TABLE OF
Contents

CHAPTER 1

Whence They Came: Departure from the Ancient Homeland

I. The First Peopling of the Americas

It has long been thought that the first people to migrate to North America came from Asia. The earliest evidence of human beings on the North American continent has been found in the regions of Alaska and the Yukon not presently covered by glaciers. These people entered the New World by crossing a dry land bridge that connected Siberia to Alaska during the time of the last major ice age. This land bridge was created when vast amounts of water became trapped as ice. As the glaciers formed, sea levels dropped by as much as one hundred metres, resulting in a very different world than the one we know today. One of the results of dropping sea levels was the creation of the land bridge known as Beringia which connected Siberia and Alaska. This land mass would have been extensive, approximately 1,600 kilometres across, ice-free and inhabited by large numbers of herd animals.

The Siberia of 18,000 years ago was a dry land with harsh, dry winters and short, hot summers. This climate produced a largely treeless landscape that received so little precipitation that it was not covered by ice during the last glacial episode. Although the archaeology of this enormous area and of northeast Asia in particular is still poorly known, it is of vital importance, because it was from these areas that the first settlement of the Americas took place.

Soviet archaeologists have identified a number of cultural traditions that existed in Siberia and northeast Asia at the same time as the land bridge between Siberia and Alaska. The cultural tradition known as the Dyukhtai seems the most likely to be that of the ancestors of the first Americans. This long-lived and ancient tradition was made up of small

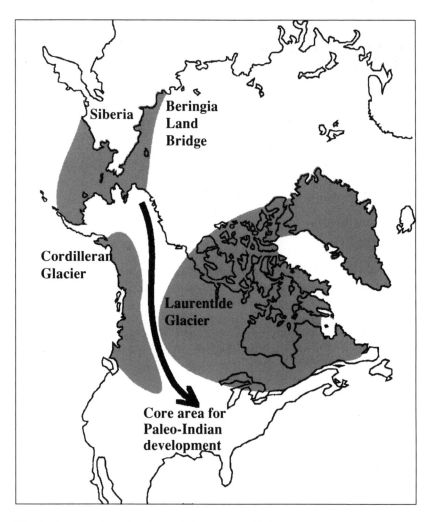

Beringia and distribution of glaciers at 12,000 years ago.

groups of hunters and gatherers who survived in an arctic environment. These people made stone spear points that were carefully flaked on both sides. For butchering tools they made tiny stone blades which are parallel-sided flakes with very sharp edges struck from a large pebble.

As big game hunters, these people would have ranged widely over a huge territory in search of their prey, camping near their kills for a few days before moving on. The herd animals they depended upon were probably the first to migrate across Beringia, and the people would have followed them into the New World.

Once in Alaska and the Yukon, these people would have been confronted with an insurmountable obstacle. At the time of the land bridge, the rest of the continent was sealed off to the migrants by two glaciers: the Continental or Laurentide glacier, which was centred in the James Bay region of Canada and moved south, and the mountain glacier which covered the Rocky Mountains and met the Laurentide glacier in the MacKenzie River Valley. These huge glaciers effectively closed off the rest of North America to the new immigrants from Asia. However, geological evidence and recent archaeological discoveries show that vast areas of Alaska and the Yukon were not covered by ice, and these areas supported the needs of the new immigrants. Once established in northwestern North America, these people remained, as the glaciers began to melt and retreat northward. The melting ice would have isolated these people in America, because as sea levels began to rise, the land bridge was covered by the Bering Sea. However, the disappearing glaciers also allowed them access to the heart of the continent, and thus a slow, southerly migration began.

The people of this time had the tools for hunting big game. They especially hunted now-extinct animal species such as mammoths, mastadons and long-horned bison, and later archaeological sites yield evidence that they hunted animals we know today.

II. Archaeology in the Maritimes

The prehistory of the Maritime peoples of eastern Canada is a difficult topic to address for a number of reasons. Principal among these, the area being considered is defined by modern political boundaries that bear little relationship to those that existed in the remote past. To complicate the issue, archaeological studies within the region have not been equally detailed. Thus, for the Maritime provinces, the prehistory of the past eleven thousand years is derived from a series of single sites representing events only at a given time and place. Although these can be discussed in a chronological order, they do not represent a continuum because, unfortunately, the Maritimes have not produced sites that were continually occupied for thousands of years. Archaeological sites that had continual human occupation are the most valuable for interpreting events of the past and are like archives for the archaeologist. As they are dug, the most recent cultural artifacts are found near the surface, and the deeper the archaeologist goes the older the material becomes. Careful excavation of such sites allows the separation of artifacts in chronological order from each level and thus reveal changes in the cultural history of the human beings who left these artifacts behind.

The table opposite is intended to provide a basic framework for a reconstruction of the prehistory of the region. The primary evidence left by prehistoric humans in the Maritime provinces is their stone artifacts. One of the difficulties faced by archaeologists is that they are restricted to evidence that has survived the tests of time. The soils of Maritime Canada are not very kind to archaeologists, because they are extremely acidic and thus it is rare that organic remains of past cultures are found. Stone resists the chemistry of the soils, being most indestructible, and therefore tools made from stone form the basis of much of the reconstructions of North American and Maritime prehistory that follow.

III. The Paleo-Indians

The big game hunting period of 8,000 to 11,000 years ago in North America has been called by archaeologists the time of the Paleo-Indians. And the cultures during the more than five thousand years of this period have been divided into three groups. The earliest is the Clovis culture, which is characterized by a chipped-stone spear point known as the

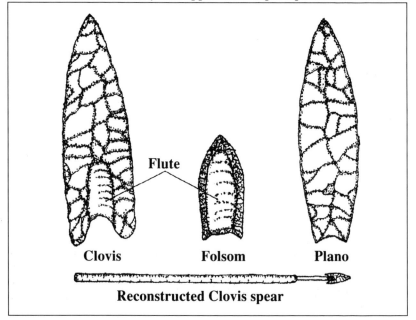

Flute

Clovis   Folsom   Plano

Reconstructed Clovis spear

Paleo-Indian spear points.

YEARS AGO	PERIOD	TRADITION	SUBSISTENCE/ SETTLEMENT PATTERNS
Present			self-determination
			reservations
	Historic	Micmac	wars against the English
			trade with Europeans
			hunting/gathering
400	Protohistoric	Etchmen	beginnings of trade
			hunting/gathering
500			hunting/gathering
	Ceramic	Maritime Woodland	coastal, seasonal
			interior activities
2500			
	Late Pre-Ceramic	Broad Point Shield Archaic	coastal, south interior, boreal forest
		Maritime Archaic Laurentian Archaic	coastal, north interior, river and lakes
5000	The Great Hiatus	Archaeological record missing	
8000	Paleo-Indian	Plano Clovis	big game hunters
11000			

Cultural chronology of the Maritime provinces.

Clovis fluted point. This culture is followed by a uniquely western North American Paleo-Indian culture known as the Folsom culture which features a fluted point of the same name. The final culture of the period is the Plano, which had a series of unfluted points.

In the western high plains area of North America, these three cultures became well established as successful hunters of big game. Meanwhile the glaciers continued to retreat northward, and the animals the Paleo-Indians relied upon moved north with them. As a result, the nomadic hunters gradually spread across the continent in all directions, and by approximately 11,000 years ago small groups of these hunters found their way into eastern Canada.

IV. The First Inhabitants of the Maritimes

Although there are many sites representative of the Paleo-Indian period in North America, only one has been excavated in the Maritimes. This site is located within the confines of the Debert Industrial Park in the general area of Truro, Nova Scotia.

This location is the oldest generally recognized and accepted site of human presence within the region. Many chipped stone tools and fluted projectile points have been found there. As mentioned, in the west of the continent two fluted point traditions are recognized: the Clovis and the Folsom. The Folsom has yet to be identified in eastern Canada and the fact that this culture was adapted to the hunting of bison (which never roamed east of the Appalachians) would suggest that remains of that culture will never be found in the Maritimes.

The Debert Paleo-Indian site is one of the most important sites of the Clovis tradition in eastern North America. Excavations at Debert revealed separate living areas associated with fireplaces and artifacts concentrations, including a wide range of Paleo-Indian tools. Stone spear points with the characteristic flutes were recovered, along with stone spokeshaves and abraders used to shape and smooth wooden spear shafts. Also found were thousands of implements used in the preparation of animal hides. The most common tool was a small stone scraper used to remove fat and hair from hides. Other tools included awls used to put holes in pieces of hide so they could be stitched together. Although no bone tools were found in the highly acidic soils of Debert, indirect evidence of their previous existence was found in the presence of special stone tools like those used to make bone implements. These included

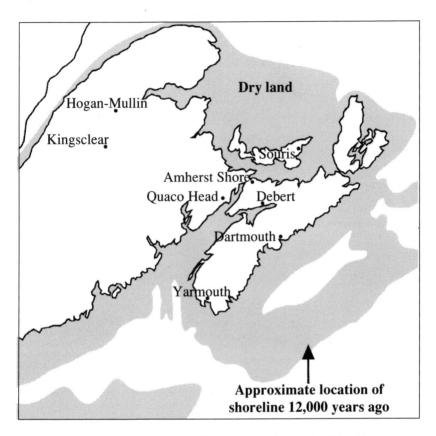

Approximate location of
shoreline 12,000 years ago

Distribution of Paleo-Indian finds throughout the Maritime provinces.

chisel-like tools and engraving tools that can cut bone into desired shapes.

Charcoal was collected from the individual hearths and dated using radiocarbon techniques, revealing an average age of 10,600± 47 years old for the site.

Although no animal remains were found during the excavations, given what we know of the paleo-environment, the site location, and the hunting strategies used elsewhere during that time, it may be that Debert was occupied by caribou hunters. The site may have been situated near a calving ground or along a caribou migration route.

And the rich ocean resources off our coast would not have been overlooked by those early people. Large wintering herds of harp seals

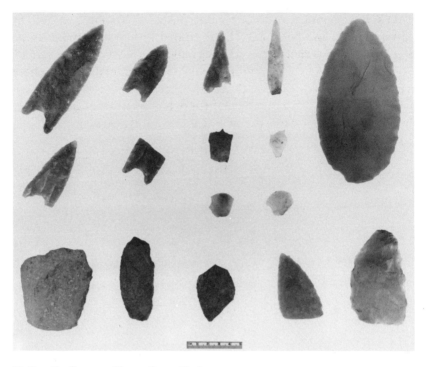

Paleo-Indian artifacts from Debert.

Saint Mary's University

may have attracted the attention of the first inhabitants. Archaeological evidence from along the coasts of southern Labrador suggests that the Paleo-Indians in this area used ocean resources. Archaeologists have concluded from studying sites in Labrador that a well defined seasonal cycle of food gathering, hunting and livelihood activities that began in this period continued through to the time of European contact.

Unfortunately, the same conclusion cannot be proven for the rest of Atlantic Canada. Whereas coastal Labrador has kept pace with rising sea levels, the coasts of the Maritime provinces have been submerging for the past 6,000 years. This means that if people did use the marine resources the evidence is now under water.

The late Paleo-Indian peoples of the Maritimes left many leaf-shaped unfluted spear points. In general, these points are long and narrow with straight sides. The points were created by pressure flaking. This techniques removes well controlled chips along the edges of the points, resulting in a series of parallel flakes. Often the base and the lower third of the point have been ground to allow the point to be fastened to a spear shaft. This grinding removes sharp projections which could cut the material used to fix the stone point onto a wooden shaft. The Plano tradition is one of the cultural periods in the Maritimes that needs a great deal more research. The scant evidence to date merely indicates that people were present in the region, but we know very little about them.

CHAPTER 2
Settling In: Adapting to the New Land

I. Introduction

The Paleo-Indians settled in the Maritimes and adapted to its resources. However, during the period after Debert was occupied the environment underwent rapid change.

Immediately following the early occupation of the Maritimes a second advance of glaciers is thought to have taken place. This movement of ice would have occurred around 10,500 years ago, and in all likelihood it forced the first peoples of the Maritimes to abandon the region. The evidence for this glaciation is found in many locations and can be detected in peat layers between 11,000 and 10,500 years old which are covered by glacially transported gravels known as till. Thus, for about 500 years, the region was not conducive to human habitation.

Beginning around 10,000 years ago, the glaciers began their final retreat. The Maritimes again experienced rapid changes in the environment, dominated by dramatic changes in sea levels. The consequences of these changes for a second migration into the region are unknown. Indeed, evidence for habitation during the period between 10,000 and 5,000 years ago is virtually non-existent. In fact this time has been labelled "The Great Hiatus" to reflect the lack of archaeological findings.

Two theories have been created to explain the missing evidence of human habitation during this time. The first theory is that the environment was completely inhospitable for human habitation. The landscape was changing so rapidly that the resources that humans would have needed to maintain themselves were unreliable and thus people chose not to live in this region.

Ground slate ulus.

Saint Mary's University

The second theory and the one thought to be most likely is that the Maritimes were occupied by people who exploited ocean resources and thus settled along the coasts of the Maritimes. Unfortunately for archaeologists, the shorelines of 10,000 to 5,000 years ago no longer exist. Their demise was related to ongoing geological events. When the glaciers were at their heights, sea levels dropped dramatically, producing very different shorelines in the Maritimes. For example, Prince Edward Island did not exist as an island but was connected to New Brunswick and Nova Scotia. As the glacier melted, the seas began to rise and covered previously dry land. Could people have lived along the now submerged shorelines during this time?

Rising sea levels could explain the lack of evidence for people in the Maritimes after the time of the human occupation at Debert. The land environment after the glaciation changed dramatically from tundra to dense boreal forests that could not have supported large mammals, thus confining food gathering and hunting activities to the ocean and shore areas. The sites occupied during this ancient period along the coast have now all been drowned.

Recent discoveries would support this notion. Scallop fishermen dragging offshore in the Bay of Fundy and along the north shore of Prince Edward Island have brought up artifacts reminiscent of an early age. These include ulus, which the Inuit cultures of the Canadian Arctic regard as women's knives. This kind of ground stone implement was used to butcher soft tissue species such as fish and sea mammals. These tools could have been lost overboard by people in canoes. However, the locations where these artifacts have been found and our knowledge of changing shorelines also strongly suggest that these tools may be from ancient but now submerged sites of human habitation.

II. Late Pre-Ceramic Period

The time from about 5,000 years ago to 2,500 years ago in the Maritimes is often called the Late Pre-Ceramic Period, which is the equivalent of what is known in other areas of North America as the Late Archaic Period. Although the evidence of humans from this period is abundant, it is also confusing. To date, no less that four broad cultural traditions have been identified, and some of these can be further subdivided into chronological phases. However, rather than trying to provide a detailed account of the differences and various debates that surround these various traditions, a general discussion will be given.

A new technology appeared in the Maritimes during this time: the production of stone tools by grinding and polishing to reach a finished form. In part this technology was introduced in response to a changed environment dominated by forests. The three most common tools from this period found throughout the Maritimes are axes, adzes and gouges, all used in woodworking. Unfortunately the Maritimes' acidic soils have not left us with direct evidence of what was being manufactured with these tools. We can only speculate that a wide variety of goods were made from wood. Were dug-out canoes made during this time? The existence of many large implements and the fact that most are found along the lakes and rivers of the Maritimes suggest the presence of some kind of water craft.

The ground stone technology was also used to produce other types of tools. Ulus have been found on land sites, notably in the southern part

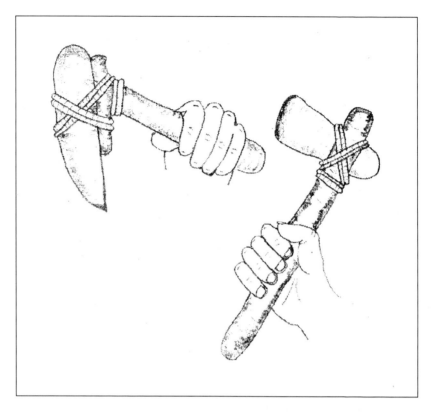

Top: Reconstructed method of lashing a gouge or adze to a wooden handle.

Bottom: Reconstructed method of lashing an axe to a wooden handle.

of Nova Scotia. The uses of two other types of artifacts from sites of this period have not been easily defined. Gorgets are flat, ground and polished implements whose function is unknown. They have a variety of shapes, and many have one or more holes drilled into them. The other mystery artifact is the plummet, which resembles a modern carpenter's plumb bob.

Some scholars have speculated that plummets were used as amulets and worn around the neck. However, this seems unlikely because many plummets are quite large and heavy. The same reasoning would dismiss their use as weights in bolas. A third idea is that they were used in fishing as sinkers for nets and lines. This notion has some credibility because many plummets have been found at locations that were good fishing spots. A final suggestion is that they are weights used to stretch rawhide. No matter what their function, plummets remain an identifying artifact for the Late Pre-Ceramic Period.

The people who produced these ground stone implements also created chipped stone tools. For the most part they used chipped stone methods to produce spear points, knives and scrapers. Of these three, the most characteristic of this period are the spear points, which tend to reflect the definitions of the four traditions mentioned earlier. The most common form has a contracted stem used to attach the point to a spear shaft.

Tools and other archaeological evidence have been used to reconstruct the activities of the Late Pre-Ceramic peoples. In all probability these people participated in a seasonal cycle of activities that included hunting, fishing and food gathering. The animals hunted include deer, moose, bear, sea mammals, smaller game and birds. Fishing was an important pursuit, with major sea-run species playing a prominent role in the people's diet during their annual migrations. Wild vegetables and nuts and berries were probably collected in season.

III. Burial Ceremonialism

To date, only one burial site from this period has been excavated in the Maritimes. It is known as the Cow Point site and is situated on the thoroughfare between Grand Lake and Maquapit Lake in central New Brunswick. The excavation of this site by the Archaeological Survey of Canada in 1971 produced 60 graves and 400 artifacts. The graves and their contents had been covered with red ochre and appear to date from two periods of time. The radiocarbon dates on the last burials average around 3,800 years old, and no dates are presently available for the earlier burials. Similar burial sites have been excavated throughout the State of Maine, where they are called the "Moorehead burial tradition."

The dead person was given either a "primary" burial with the body in an extended or flexed position, or a "secondary" burial in which his or her separated bones were placed in a bundle, These two types of interments are evidence that the location of cemeteries were important to the members of the culture that used them. The primary burials represent people who died reasonably near the cemetery in a season when their graves could be easily dug. The secondary, or bundle, burials represent members of the group who died at some distance from the cemetery or in the winter when they could not be buried because of snow cover and frozen ground. The remains of the deceased would have been left until they could be gathered up, placed in a bundle covered by skins or bark, and taken to the cemetery for burial.

The presence of the red ochre and particular sets of grave goods—most often, ground stone items—suggests a degree of ceremonialism. The rare instances where bones of the dead have been analyzed as to age and sex have revealed no distinctions in types of grave goods for different individuals. Thus the objects in the graves were probably deposited by members of the community and were not necessarily the possessions of the deceased. Indeed, most of the objects appear to be non-utilitarian and ceremonial in nature. This suggests that they were perhaps not meant to be used as tools in another life after death.

No cemeteries have been excavated in Nova Scotia or on Prince Edward Island. However, many of the private collections in Nova Scotia viewed by the author contain the unique grave goods associated with the same type of ceremonialism. In many instances the artifacts still have red ochre stains and the collectors remembered the presence of oval patches of red stained soil in the place where they found the objects.

The most intriguing grave goods recovered in the cemeteries are called "bayonets." The name is derived from their shapes, which closely resemble a World War I rifle bayonet. These stone "bayonets" are made from ground slate and have been found in a variety of sizes and forms. In many cases, they have incised geometric lines on one or both faces. These decorated pieces seem to be much too fragile to have served a utilitarian function. However, thicker bayonets made from slate and bone have also been found and could have been used as the tips of spears or lances. A third type, which is fairly common in collections from southwestern Nova Scotia, has a small stemmed form. These have a unique way of being attached to a wooden spear shaft. The stems have a groove grounded into them that resembles a flute. The presence of this hafting technique should not be considered a link with the fluting technology found in Paleo-Indian points. It is merely a reintroduction of a technique that helped its maker to secure this type of point to a spear or lance.

The presence of burial ceremonialism in Maine and the Maritime provinces has been the focus of much archaeological debate. In fact, the cemeteries of the "Red Paint People" have compounded the problem because, to date, few habitation sites can be linked to this unique burial pattern; thus the archaeological community has concentrated on the cemeteries. All cultures are made up of various components, including disposal of the dead, annual subsistence pursuits, and various forms of social organization, to name a few. If we attempt to define an entire culture by merely looking at one of the components, then our archaeological reconstructions are suspect. At this time, the burial sites of these people must be viewed as what they were—repositories of the dead and not representative of an entire way of life.

IV. Ceramic Period

Typically, the shift from one cultural period to another can be seen in marked changes in the archaeological record. It has long been recognized that this is not the case for the Maritime provinces of eastern Canada. The grey, transitional time between the end of the Late Pre-Ceramic Period and the beginning of the full Ceramic Period remains an enigma for archaeologists. One main problem is our lack of excavated sites with evidence of continual human habitation over these time periods. This problem is compounded by the strong possibility that cultures from other regions may be responsible for at least some of the changes seen in the archaeological record. However, it can be said that the introduction of pottery in the lives of the Maritime peoples signals the end of the Pre-Ceramic Period and the beginning of the last major cultural events before European contact.

The Ceramic Period began approximately 2,500 years ago and lasted for two thousand years. Unfortunately, at this time the archaeological evidence has yet to be adequately studied to provide a detailed sequence for the changing styles of ceramic technology. So this era in the Maritimes is still divided into three broad periods labelled Early, Middle and Late.

V. Early Ceramic Period

The Early Ceramic Period is characterized by clay vessels with cord impressions on the interior and exterior. These decorations are achieved by wrapping a stick with cord and impressing it onto the vessel walls while the clay is still relatively soft. The result is a series of oval impressions left by the cord. This kind of decoration characterizes what is known elsewhere as the Vinette family of pottery.

The presence of Vinette ceramics in a dateable context within the Maritimes remains a high probability. Two fragments recently came to light in a collection gathered by John Erskine from a site in the Gaspereau Valley of Nova Scotia, and others have been found on the Spednik Lakes in New Brunswick. Using these fragments and the broad range of dates from outside the Maritimes, a median date of 2,500 years ago can be assigned to the beginnings of ceramic technology in the Maritimes. Shortly after this date a unique cultural event took place in the Maritimes—a foreign ritual was introduced.

Significant archaeological sites are often discovered under unusual circumstances. In early June 1986 one such discovery was made. An architect, Mr. Jan Skora, while jogging with his wife in a newly developed subdivision on the outskirts of Halifax, Nova Scotia, happened along a recently bulldozed access road. His fortuitous journey, along with his professional interest in potential building sites for his clients, combined with some early training in archaeology received in his native Poland, drew his attention to a large knoll overlooking Prospect Bay. Half of the knoll had fallen victim to the bulldozers that had cut it away to fill in the roadbed and adjoining building lots.

Mr. Skora's attention was drawn to a dark soil stain exposed on the top of the knoll. He left the road and climbed the hill to investigate the stain and was immediately rewarded with the discovery of several stone artifacts. His enthusiasm and his training in archaeology led him to report his finds to the agency responsible for archaeology in the province, the Nova Scotia Museum.

In the two years following his discovery, the Nova Scotia Museum and Saint Mary's University conducted excavations at this location, which has been named the Skora site. From this archaeological work we now know that the hill was a sanctuary for the dead. It contained a number of burials that were treated in a unique fashion. The bodies were first cremated and then the remains were gathered up and placed in small shallow pits on top of the hill. In one instance a group of artifacts had been placed in a grave and then cremated; afterwards, more objects were placed in the same grave. This activity produced charcoal that has been dated to approximately 2,400 years ago.

The burial ritual did not end with the placement of the human remains in their graves. The final act was to cover all of them with a

Ceramic Period artifacts.

Saint Mary's University

mound of dirt. This type of treatment of the dead is known at only one other site in the Maritimes, located on the Red Bank reserve in northern New Brunswick. This kind of burial ceremonialism is a unique cultural activity which may have had its origin in the Illinois and Ohio river valleys of central North America. How it arrived in the Maritimes remains one of the intriguing questions in the cultural history of the region.

VI. Middle and Late Ceramic Periods

The archaeological record for the Middle and Late Ceramic periods has been primarily defined from "shell midden" sites found along the coasts of the Maritimes. Shell middens are accumulations of discarded molluscs—clams, quohogs, mussels and occasionally scallops and oysters. The aboriginal inhabitants, beginning approximately two thousand years ago, began to use these resources exposed by the falling tides. The presence of mollusc remains is a bonus for archaeologists working in this region of Canada. The discarded shells are rich in calcium, which acts as a neutralizing agent in the normally acidic soils of the Maritimes. As a result, organic remains such as food bone and tools made from bone are often preserved amongst the shells.

Shell middens have attracted the attention of various scholars throughout the history of archaeology in the area. Indeed, the first professionally conducted excavations in the early part of this century were on middens at Mahone Bay and Merigomish Harbour, Nova Scotia. The fascination with this type of site has continued into modern times with the excavation of dozens of middens in all three Maritime provinces.

Although a great deal of effort has been directed towards identifying the material culture represented in middens, very little is known about why and how Native peoples began to exploit molluscs. It may be that this substantial resource was introduced to them by immigrants to the area. A counter suggestion would be that they discovered the resource through their own inquisitiveness and exploration. The answer to this problem may be found in the remains of a small site at Smiths Cove in Digby County, Nova Scotia. This location was excavated in the summer of 1975 and proved to be an early Middle Ceramic Period short-term habitation. Although only a few artifacts were recovered to support the date of the site (about 2,000 years old), the structure of the midden was of interest. It was primarily composed of a thin paste made up of the remains of the common blue mussel (*Mytilus edulis*). This may suggest that, in the initial period of shellfish gathering for food, the most easily seen and harvested mollusc species were eaten. The blue mussel is easily collected from intertidal zones, where it is found in clusters attached to various rocks and outcrops. Far less effort is required to gather this species than to dig for clams (*Mya arenaria*). However, local mussels are depleted more quickly and require more time to re-establish themselves than do the species of clams that are found in this same area.

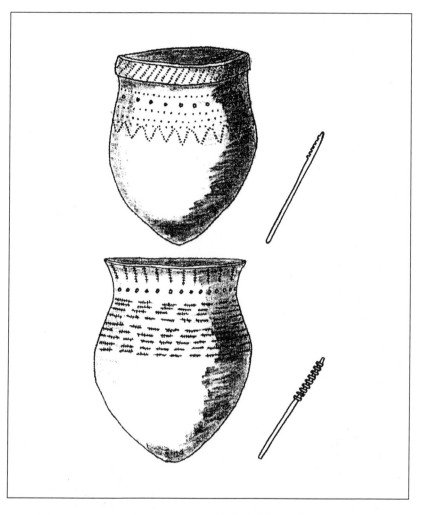

Top: Dentate-stamped vessel from Middle Ceramic.
Bottom: Cord-marked vessel from Late Ceramic.

Thus one could speculate that people were drawn to the mussel beds first and, when they became depleted, efforts were directed at collecting the other species buried in the mud.

It may be useful to look at a single midden that spans the Middle and Late Ceramic periods. The site that best exemplifies this is the Sellar's Cove site located on the northeast side of St. Margaret's Bay, Nova Scotia. This site had received attention from an amateur who "excavated" it in an uncontrolled fashion during the summer of 1960. Although a few notes from this work are available, all of the specimens have been lost. Fortunately, his activities were restricted to a small pocket of eroding midden on the southeast end of the site. Once this pocket had been removed, he concluded that he had explored the entire undisturbed portion of the site. He reported that the remainder of the habitation area was not worthy of investigation as it had been ploughed under to produce a pasture.

Excavations were undertaken at this location in the summer of 1977 by a crew of students from Saint Mary's University. They discovered that not only had the size of the site been underestimated but that the cultural deposit under the ploughed zone was relatively undisturbed. Their efforts produced hundreds of artifacts from the site, including pottery representing the Middle and Late Ceramic periods.

The Middle Ceramic Period vessels found at Sellar's Cove were characterized by thin-walled pots decorated by a fine dentate stamping technique. This decoration results when a notched tool is applied to the soft clay. The impressions left are rectangular or square, resembling the teeth of a comb. Many bone stamping tools were also recovered from the lower levels of this midden site. The earliest occupants of Sellar's Cove also produced chipped stone spear points with expanding bases for attachment to spear shafts, These artifacts, along with a variety of barbed bone and antler fishing implements, combine to form the basic tool kits typical of the Middle Ceramic phrase.

The upper levels of the midden represent the Late Ceramic phase in the Maritimes. In general, the clay pots show a decline in quality. They are thicker walled and less attention was paid to their manufacture. The decoration has once again been done with a cord-wrapped stick, but designs appear on the outside of the vessels only.

These pots are associated with small chipped-stone projectile points that have been notched to form an expanding stem for hafting. The sizes of the points indicate that they were probably used as arrowheads—thus we can conclude that the use of the bow and arrow in the Maritimes arose during the Late Ceramic Period. As in the lower levels of the midden, a variety of fishing tools made from bone and antler were found. A rather unique specimen, a section of a necklace made from rolled copper beads, was also found in these upper levels. The Ceramic Period ends with the coming of Europeans to the Maritimes.

CHAPTER 3
History in the Maritimes

I. The Protohistoric and Historic Periods

The Europeans who came to the New World created the first written records that identify the aboriginal peoples of the Maritimes by name. The French colonials identified two groups of people in what they called Acadia: the Souriquois and the Etechemin. With the defeat of the French and the entry of the English, the people known as the Souriquois began to be called the Micmac. The name Micmac comes from the word *nikmaq*, which means "my kin-friends." *Nikmaq* was a form of greeting used by the Micmac in the early seventeenth century and became associated with the people themselves. In later years the spelling took its common modern form. The territories occupied by the Micmac included Nova Scotia, Prince Edward Island, and most of New Brunswick north and east of the St. John River.

The language of the Micmac is part of the Eastern Algonquin family and has close affinities with the language unit called the Micmac-Maleseet-Passamaquoddy. The latter two languages were also prevalent within New Brunswick during the seventeenth century and were found in an area that was formerly identified with the people known by the French as the Etechemin.

With the arrival of the Europeans, the region entered into the Historic Period. The seventeenth century brought explorers, missionaries, adventurers and merchants to the shores of the Maritimes. Some of these early visitors gained an intimate knowledge of the Native peoples and recorded their observations and views. One of the earliest accounts of the Micmac was written by Marc Lescarbot, who arrived at Port Royal in 1606 and stayed for one year. During this time he travelled to the St. John

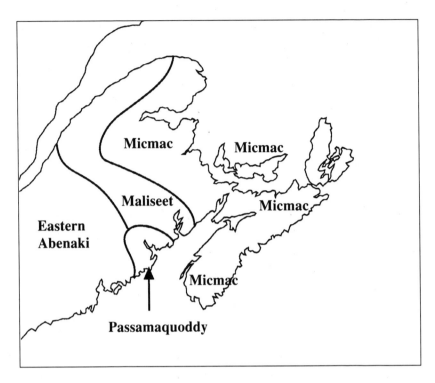

Distribution of historic tribes within the Maritime provinces, c. 1700.

River area and paid a visit to the ruins of the first unsuccessful European settlement on St. Croix Island. After returning to France, Lescarbot published a number of short works, culminating in his *History of New France* published in French in 1609. This work contained many references to the Micmac and their ways of life.

The author who wrote the most explicitly about the activities of the Micmac was Father Pierre Biard, who arrived in Port Royal with the expressed purpose of bringing Christianity to the native populations. His stay was short-lived, however, because he was captured by the English in 1613 and deported back to France. His translated writings, *Relation of New France, and the Jesuit Father's Voyage to that Country* have been published as part of the *Jesuit Relations*.

The author who spend the longest time in the New World was Nicolas Denys, who arrived in 1632 and spent nearly forty years in the Maritimes. Throughout his stay he moved about between various land grants, becoming involved in the fishery, fur trade, lumbering and government of Acadia. Although his book, *Description and Natural History of the Coasts of North America*, was written from memory when he was seventy-two years old, it is believed to be accurate in most of its content.

The final major early contributor to writings in a European language on the customs of the Native peoples was Chretien Le Clercq, a Recollect missionary who arrived in late 1675. His book, *New Relations of Gaspesia*, written in 1691, was an intimate account of his twelve years living and travelling with the Micmac of the north shore of New Brunswick and Cape Breton Island.

These early writers left vivid accounts of the lifestyles of the Micmac during the seventeenth century. They provided many descriptions of how various animals were hunted, and also give accounts of the many material possessions of the Micmac and their methods of cooking and constructing shelters. Thus, although the earlier chapters in this book had to rely solely on archaeological evidence to reconstruct the events of the past, from this point onward historical documents have been used as well.

All of the seventeenth-century accounts report that certain animals and other food sources were obtained during specific times of the year. In his book, Father Biard provided a summary of the seasonal round:

> In January they have the seal-hunting: For this animal, although it is aquatic, nevertheless spawns upon certain islands about this time. . . .
>
> In the month of February and until the middle of March, is the great hunt for beavers, otters, moose, bears (which are very good), and for the caribou, an animal half ass and half deer. In the middle of March, fish begin to spawn, and to come up from the sea with certain streams, often so abundantly that everything swarms with them. . . .
>
> Among these fish the smelt is the first; this smelt is two or three times as large as in our rivers; after the smelt comes the herring at the end of April; and at the same time bustards, which are large ducks, double the size of ours, come from the south. . . . At the same time comes the sturgeon, and salmon, and the great search through the Islets for eggs, as the waterfowl, which are there in great numbers, lay their eggs then. . . . From the month of May up to the middle of September, they are free from

all anxiety about their food; for the cod are upon the coast, and all kinds of fish and shellfish; and the French ship with which they traffic. . . . Now our savages in the middle of September withdraw from the sea, beyond the reach of the tides, to the little rivers, where the eels spawn, of which they lay in a supply for they are good and fat. In October and November comes the second hunt for elks and beaver; and then in December (wonderful providence of God) comes a fish called by them *ponamo* [tomcod] which spawns under the ice.

The methods used by the Micmac to capture their food resources varied with the seasons. During the summer, beaver were stalked on land, or in the water from a canoe. The killing implements included spears and arrows. A more industrious technique was to break the beavers' dam, draining their ponds and killing them as they attempted to escape.

The winter hunt for beaver also required a good deal of work on the part of the hunters. The ice on the ponds would be broken in forty or fifty places. Then the Micmac would break the dams and beaver lodges to cause the animals to flee to one of the openings, where they could be caught. Sometimes the ice and lodges would simply be struck with large poles to drive the beaver to the edges of the frozen ponds. The Micmac would then locate the prey with the help of their dogs, cut the ice and remove the beavers.

The great efforts put into the beaver hunt by the Micmac that are described in the seventeenth-century reports came as a result of the fur trade. The beaver was the most sought-after fur bearer because its pelt was a valuable trade item.

The moose was the most productive food animal for the Micmac and played an important role in their economy. This animal was hunted throughout the year by hunters with the aid of dogs. However, the most successful time to hunt moose was from February through mid-March. Then, under ideal conditions, the moose could be tracked in soft, deep snow while the hunter pursued it with the help of his dogs and snowshoes. The moose tired easily in the deep snow, whereas the hunter wearing snowshoes could travel across the surface without sinking. The moose was dispatched with arrows or a spear while the dogs surrounded it and hindered it from escaping.

Fishing was also an important seasonal activity. Large species such

Spring fishing.

Teresa MacPhee

as sturgeon and salmon were taken with an implement called a leister, a three-pronged spear with a central point flanked by two barbed points. A large fish is impaled on the centre point and held in place by the barbed points. A smaller version of the leister was also used on arrows to shoot flying birds.

The Micmac also employed various traps for catching fish. These included nets and loosely woven baskets set in streams that were dammed with rocks or poles to force the fish into them.

Migrating waterfowl played an important role in the diet of the Micmac each spring. Denys recorded a particularly effective technique for taking a large number of ducks in a single evening. At night the hunters would lie down in a canoe and aim it to drift into a flock of ducks. When the Micmac were amongst the birds, they would light birchbark torches and hold them over their heads. This move surprised and confused the sleeping ducks, which took flight but circled the torches, allowing the hunters to knock them down with long poles. Denys reported that in a single night two or three hunters could fill a canoe by using this technique.

Summer camp.

The most common method for cooking meat was to roast it over an open fire by placing cuts of game on a sharpened stick or on a grill made from split sticks. One of the most interesting aspects of Micmac cooking was their method of boiling food. By the time of European contact the Micmac had stopped making clay pots. Their principal containers were then made from birchbark stitched with spruce roots and sealed along the seams with spruce gum. These containers were watertight and could be used in many ways, including for cooking. The container was suspended over the fire above the flame, and heated rocks were removed from the fire with wooden tongs and placed in the birchbark "pot" until they cooled. This was done again and again until the contents boiled.

An intriguing possession of the Micmac that was described by all of the early writers was their wooden kettle. Wooden kettles were fashioned from large sections of logs that were hollowed out using fire and stone axes. The top of the log was burned and then the soft ashes and burnt wood were removed with an axe, the maker taking care not to burn or cut through the sides. Once the kettle was hollowed out, it could be filled with water and, using the same technique employed with the bark

Petroglyph.

Teresa MacPhee

Petroglyph from the Historic Period.

containers, the water could be brought to a boil. The most common use of the kettle was in the production of *cacamos*, or moose butter. After a moose was butchered, its bones were broken up and put into a wooden kettle full of boiling water. The fat and marrow in the bones would rise to the top, where it was scooped out with a wooden spoon. A single moose would yield five to six pounds of this highly nutritional butter.

The animals not only provided food, but other essential items were manufactured from their skins, bones and antlers. Bones and antlers provided raw materials for many of the tools used by the Micmac. These included the bone points on leisters, needles used in sewing clothing, pins used to secure clothing, and many other items.

Animal skins were tanned and used for clothing and containers and as trade items. Both men and women wore loincloths, leggings, sleeves and moccasins. In the winter every individual might wear a beaverskin robe. The different items of apparel were carefully sewn with bone or copper needles, and with thread often made from the dried back sinew of animals. Often the clothing and accessories were decorated by painting or by the addition of patterns of dyed porcupine quills. The

Historic Micmac camp.

dyes for the quills and paint came from naturally occurring pigments such as red and yellow ochre. The color white came from grinding up shells, and black was derived from charcoal.

The decorations included geometric designs such as parallel lines, triangles and circles. One of the more aesthetically pleasing designs is the uniquely Micmac "double-curve" motif. This design element has been found amongst the petroglyphs in Kejimkujik National Park in Nova Scotia.

The Micmac of the seventeenth century constructed houses made from poles covered with birchbark sewn together with spruce roots. Their houses included a number of different shapes, with the most common being the conical wigwam. This type of construction was ideal for the Micmac because it was not only warm and comfortable but was easily erected and completely portable. The strips of bark were light-

History in the Maritimes   **31**

weight and could be rolled up and carried to the next campsite. The Micmac decorated their houses with images painted on the bark. Inside the wigwam was a central fireplace bordered with stone. The smoke from the fire could escape through the opening at the top where the framing poles met. The floor was covered with fir boughs, which in turn were covered with woven reed mats and animal skins.

The natural resources of the Maritimes and the Native people's adaptation to them provided a lifestyle in harmony with the environment. This way of life came to an end after the arrival of the Europeans. The Micmac were among the first Native peoples in North America to become actively involved with permanent European settlements on the continent. The accelerated contact, as more and more Europeans arrived, resulted in dramatic cultural changes for the Micmac. This was particularly true of their economic activities and relationships. They quickly moved from an economy that maintained a healthy resident population to one that needed European "handouts" and technologies for survival. The disruption to the Native people's way of life as it had been established over a period of ten thousand years was complete. Although the population was not replaced, it was decimated by European diseases and was dominated by foreign technologies and later by the sheer numbers of Europeans.

The history of the Micmac during colonial times was closely intertwined with that of the major powers. During the first hundred years when the French and Acadians began to settle throughout the Maritimes, the Micmac remained an independent people. Early European settlements were confined to coastal regions or found along the marshlands of the principal rivers. For the Micmac such communities could be ignored because they did not hinder the traditional way of life. Rather than entering into conflicts, the Micmac chose to cooperate with the French. Trading relationships grew and French missionaries were accepted. A growing dependence on French goods and conversions to Catholicism led to natural alliances with the French.

The eighteenth century was a time of political turmoil between France and England in Europe. These conflicts spread to the New World and many battles were fought on the shores and waters of the Maritime Provinces. In 1710 a British force successfully captured Port Royal. With the signing of the Treaty of Utrecht in 1713, most of the former French colony of Acadia was turned over to Great Britain, while the French still maintained Ile Royale (Cape Breton Island) and Ile Saint-

Jean (Prince Edward Island). The uneasy quality of the peace was heightened by large numbers of military personnel being based throughout the Maritimes as the Micmac territory rose in importance for the European powers.

The French reinforced Louisbourg, and the British established a strong military presence at Halifax in 1749. This growing dominance by the British and their New England allies lead to resistance by the Micmac. This resistance was in part an attempt by the Micmac to restore their valued economic relationship with the French and was reinforced by their adopted religion. Throughout this period both powers cemented their holds on territory by bringing in large numbers of immigrants. When Cornwallis established Halifax, he brought with him more than 2,500 settlers and this number swelled to 5,000 in the following year.

With the growing European population, the Micmac could no longer ignore intrusions on their homeland, They resisted by allying themselves with the French during the various military conflicts. Despite temporary truces with the British, the Micmac considered themselves at war against an occupying power. They conducted successful raids against British settlers and virtually held Haligonians captive in their own city during the first three years of its existence.

Although the Micmac considered their military activities to be a legitimate enterprise to free their lands from an intruding force, the British and the settlers they brought to the Maritimes recognized the Micmac as hostiles. Fear of the Micmac caused a bounty to be offered for every Indian scalped or captured alive, no matter whether man, woman or child.

Continued hostilities between the French and Micmac on one hand and the British and New Englanders on the other led to a major event in Maritime history. Beginning in August 1755 all Acadian inhabitants of the region were to be expelled. The loss of the Acadians and the capture of Ile Royale and Ile Saint-Jean by the British effectively ended the French influence in the region. Thus by the 1760s the Micmac were virtually on their own as the only people who had opposed the British in the Maritimes. Their chiefs signed a treaty of peace in 1761 in the hope that a relationship similar to the one they had had with the French would be established with the British. Once again historic events beyond Micmac control ruled their future destiny. The American Revolution forced the British to lose most of their North American colonies, which led to a reinforcement of the military in Halifax, the last

Micmac veterans.

strategic base of the English on the east coast. It also brought an influx of thousands of Loyalist refugees throughout the Maritimes. The end result was that the Micmac were rapidly dispossessed of what remaining lands they held.

The large numbers of settlers led in 1783 to a new political structure for the former Micmac territory. The region was divided into three colonies: Nova Scotia, New Brunswick and Prince Edward Island. Thus, although generally all under British control, the Micmac became fragmented as a people and their rights were left in the hands of colonial governments. This situation prevailed until the Maritime region became, through Confederation, part of the Dominion of Canada. The responsibility for aboriginal peoples was passed from colonial to federal authority, but this change had little early effect on the Micmac as Ottawa was preoccupied with establishing its presence in western Canada.

The late nineteenth century brought rapid industrialization throughout Canada. The development of railways, coal mines, lumbering and many small industries in the Maritimes led to a short period of prosperity, and the Micmac shared in these good times. However, after the turn of the century came economic collapse and the beginnings of the east being labelled as the poorest part of Canada.

Political intrigues in Europe offered an opportunity for the Micmac to escape this poverty. During the First World War 150 Micmac males enlisted, including every eligible Micmac male in Sydney and half of the adult Native males on Prince Edward Island. With the onset of the Second World War, Micmac people were employed in industries and on farms to help the war effort, and about 250 men joined various branches of the armed forces. Later, the call to arms was answered by 60 Micmac during the Korean conflict.

The employment situation on the reserves for returning veterans was bleak, so many sought work in the United States. Jay's Treaty of 1794 permitted free movement of Native peoples across the Canada-U.S. border. Boston was and remains the city of choice for many Micmac who seek to improve their economic positions. Entire families have migrated to Boston, with some returning to retire and live out their lives on various Reserves.

II. Conclusion

The aboriginal peoples of the Maritimes share a long and complex cultural history. The archaeological record places the first inhabitants of the region here approximately 11,000 years ago. The material remains in ancient sites show how cultures changed in response to different environments throughout the millenia. The coming of the Europeans drastically altered the former lifeways of the Native population and the traditional Micmac culture. Historic contributions by the Micmac, prominent individuals among them, and the modern issues facing this people are discussed in the remaining chapters of this book.

CHAPTER 4

Contributions to the Maritimes and Canada

I. The Welcoming

The Native people had a long and successful cultural history in the Maritimes before the arrival of the Europeans. Through the millenia they had adapted to the diversity of the ecological zones of the region and gained an intimate knowledge of its various natural resources. The first Europeans to reach the shores of the Maritimes came only on a seasonal basis, arriving in their tall ships to exploit the rich schools of fish found offshore. The necessity to dry the fish onshore brought them into contact with the Micmac. These first encounters were peaceful and an early exchange network was established. The Micmac provided the fishermen with fresh meat and furs in exchange for European manufactured goods. In part, this relationship accelerated European interest in the Maritimes. In fact, it may be said that the peaceful association and helpfulness of the Micmac towards these early visitors encouraged the colonization of the region.

The first permanent settlements in the Maritimes were those established by the French. The ill-fated De Monts occupation on St. Croix Island in 1604 was replaced by the more successful habitation of Port Royal in 1605. The misery felt by the French through the winters was partially alleviated by supplies of food given them by the Micmac. This relationship of good will was apparent in the participation of the sagamore (chief) Membertou in the "Order of Good Cheer." Unfortunately, the aboriginal attitude of caring for the well-being of one's fellows was to prove disastrous for the Micmac.

The coming of the Europeans had three major negative effects on Micmac culture. The early historical records show that what most concerned the Micmac was the increased number of deaths from epidemic disease. Although pre-contact population figures are uncertain, estimates are that the aboriginal population declined by about 80 to 90 percent as a result of disease within the first century after contact.

The second major threat to Micmac culture brought about by contact was the disruption of their subsistence and economic system. Prior to the arrival of the Europeans, each community had been self-sufficient in providing for its members. Food was shared among all of the people by the successful hunters, usually through the headman. With the establishment of the fur trade, this aspect of Micmac culture broke down. Individual hunters desirous of manufactured goods from across the Atlantic became competitive. Further, through direction from the European traders, the traditional food animals were not hunted as often but more emphasis was placed on the trapping of fur bearers. The insatiable demand for these animals quickly led to their overexploitation, effectively destroying the fur trade in the Maritimes even before it began in the rest of Canada.

Although the economic usefulness of the Micmac to the Europeans declined with the failing trade in furs, the French still had a need for allies in their wars against the English. The contest for European control of North America involved the participation of many Native peoples, including the Micmac. The relationships established during the first hundred or so years of contact with the French naturally led the Micmac to their side of the conflicts. And, as allies, they suffered the consequences of the French defeats at the hands of the British.

II. Contributions to Canadian Material Culture

At the time of European contact, the Micmac peoples of the Maritimes had successfully adapted to a wide range of environmental conditions. Some adaptations that became not only a part of the early history but continue to contribute to modern society are those associated with various forms of transportation. The three major items used throughout eastern Canada by the Micmac and other Native peoples that were quickly adopted by Europeans were the canoe, the toboggan and the snowshoe.

The history of the bark canoe in the Maritimes prior to the coming of the Europeans is poorly known. The problem is that these watercraft were made with highly perishable materials. Remarkable conditions

Petroglyph from the Historic Period.

would be required for even the smallest portion of a canoe to be preserved at an archaeological site. The only possible evidence of their existence prior to the coming of the Europeans is found in rock carvings at Kejimkujik National Park. However, even these may date to the Historic Period.

The earliest historical records, dating back to the times of Jacques Cartier, contain vague descriptions of canoes. Although lacking in detail, these records support the idea that the canoe was a highly developed technology that must have been in existence prior to the first appearance of the Europeans. The writings of early explorers contain expressions of admiration for the Native people's skill in construction and use of the canoe. The Europeans were most impressed with the fact that the canoe was built of bark over a lightweight wooden frame. They also often remarked on the speed of the canoe and its load-carrying capacity in shallow water.

Diverse environmental conditions and a variety of needs led the Micmac to build four different types of canoes. The smallest was the hunting canoe, which ranged in size from 9 to 14 feet (3 to 4.5 metres). This light craft was designed to traverse the shallow streams of the Maritimes, and its weight allowed it to be easily carried from one stream to the next. The second model was used in larger rivers and lakes of the Micmac territory and is called the "big river canoe." Its design was identical to that of the hunting canoe, but its length ranged from 15 to 20 feet (5 to 6.5 metres).

The Micmac canoe that most impressed the Europeans was the large "open water canoe." This vessel ranged from 18 to 24 feet (6 to 8.5 metres) in length and was used for hunting large sea mammals off the shores of the Maritimes. This type of canoe was seen by Cartier in 1534 at Prince Edward Island and in the Bay of Chaleur. The fourth model was the "war canoe," about which little is known other than it was the same length as the "open water" type, but sharper and with less beam to allow for faster speed.

The distinctive characteristics of Micmac canoes are their raised midsections and their generally rounded bows and sterns. In early historic times, the Micmac type of canoe was found as far south as New England. It is thought to have been brought there by Micmac war parties involved in the Abenaki conflicts against the English. Today, the thousands of recreational canoes found across Canada can trace their origins back to those of the Native people of North America.

Travel in winter snow was made easier by the use of snowshoes and by pulling one's belongings on a toboggan or sled. The name toboggan is the English equivalent of the Micmac word *tabagan*. These were constructed of a single slab of wood that was turned up in the front and held by two thongs attached to the body. The Micmac toboggan, in early contact times, ranged in width from a foot and a half to two feet (50 to 70 centimetres), was six to eight feet long (1.8 to 2.4 metres) and about one half inch (2 centimetres) thick.

The distinctive aspect of the Micmac snowshoe is its square toe (the front border is almost straight). Women and children tended to use light-framed snowshoes, and men used heavier ones. The snow conditions also dictated size: the largest were used on light powdery snow, and the smallest on snow with a hard crust. All were constructed of a wooden hoop frame with two wooden crosspieces. The toe and heel sections

Historic Period stone pipes.

Saint Mary's University

were filled in with thongs of moose or caribou rawhide. These were netted using a large bone needle with a hole in the centre. Such tools have been found in Ceramic Period shell middens, suggesting that the snowshoe has been a part of Micmac culture for thousands of years.

The canoe, the toboggan and the snowshoe have been highlighted here because they represent Micmac technologies that have been adapted by Europeans and continue in use to this day. The Micmac have also contributed a rich cultural tradition that helps make the Maritimes a unique region in Canada. The museums of the three Maritime provinces contain many examples of the prehistory and history of the Micmac. The objects in these museums range from relatively simple stone tools to complicated woven baskets and quillwork boxes. These latter objects were produced as trade goods and are still available in the many Micmac

owned and operated craft shops throughout the Maritimes.

III. Oral Tradition, Legends and Names

Although the Micmac did not have a written language prior to the coming of the Europeans, they did have a rich oral tradition. Their many myths, legends and stories have been handed down through the generations. These have been collected by people such as the Reverend Silas T. Rand, who served as a missionary among the Micmac for forty years. His records of Micmac oral tradition was first published in 1894 under the title of *Legends of the Micmacs*. Other individuals have also collected and published stories that have formed the basis for children's storybooks and anthologies written for adults.

A principal character in many of these stories is the Micmac cultural hero "Glooscap" (other spellings include Gluskap and Kluskap). To him are attributed many of the worldly possessions of the Micmac, including the canoe. One of Glooscap's supernatural powers was the ability to transform objects and living things into stone. As a result, many places throughout the Maritimes where strangely shaped rocks are present are associated with stories involving Glooscap.

One such story is related to a modern event—the proposed rock quarry development on Kelly's Mountain in Cape Breton Island. This quarry site is near Fairy Hole cave, which for generations of the Micmac has been associated with Glooscap. The stories about this cave describe it as Glooscap's final home when he left the Earth World behind. One of the three large rocks in front of the cave is identified as Glooscap's table. This rock has served as a place where the Micmac could leave offerings to Glooscap, their spirit-helper. The association of the cave with Glooscap is the central reason why the Micmac are opposed to the development of the quarry.

A short distance from the cave lie the Bird Islands, which are associated with a legend involving a battle between Glooscap and an evil wizard. The wizard was extremely jealous of the respect the Micmac had for Glooscap's magic, so he plotted to kill Glooscap. One day the wizard kidnapped two girls and stole Glooscap's stone canoe. As he paddled into St. Ann's Bay, he taunted Glooscap to rescue the girls, Glooscap suddenly appeared next to the canoe and he carried the girls to safety. He returned and, lifting the stone canoe, threw it and the wizard into the bay. The Bird Islands are identified by Micmac oral tradition as the remains of Glooscap's stone canoe.

This abbreviated version of a Micmac legend is but one of many such stories that have enriched Canadian culture. It is fortunate for today's society that Silas Rand and others have taken the interest to preserve the oral traditions of the Micmac. Without their contributions, a valuable element of aboriginal culture would have been lost forever.

The cultural history of the Maritimes has also been preserved by the various geographical place names bearing Micmac words. In most instances the original spelling has changed over the years. However, even today tourists to the Maritimes are tongue-tied by names such as those that appear below along with their original meanings:

Tatamagouche	"barred across the entrance with sand"
Musquodoboit	"rolling out in foam"
Miminegash	"portage place"
Miscouche	"little marshy place"

Kouchibouguac   "long tideway river"

Nepisiquit   "the river that dashes roughly along."

IV. Publications

The monthly newspaper known as the *Micmac News* celebrated its twentieth year of publication in 1989. This newspaper has made a very significant contribution to life in the Maritimes by providing a forum for the open expression of ideas and opinions within the Micmac community, and by serving as a vehicle for the conveyance of important information about Micmac culture to the rest of society.

The attempts of the Micmac to establish a published forum for communication among themselves and with others date back to 1932, when the late Chief Ben E. Christmas first published a short-lived newspaper. The effort was revived in 1966 when Roy Gould and Noel Doucette began a newspaper in cooperation with the Extension Department of St. Francis Xavier University that was funded as a community project but lasted only six months until the program's funds expired.

The white paper of 1969 in which the Trudeau Liberal government proposed to repeal the Indian Act of 1851 led to resistance and unprecedented unity among all Native groups across Canada. The spirit of Indian nationalism expressed itself in Nova Scotia with the formation of the Union of Nova Scotia Indians with Noel Doucette as its first president and Roy Gould as coordinator of communications. The need to inform the membership of the Union's activities was fulfilled by the reintroduction of the *Micmac News*.

This newspaper remained an information vehicle for the Union of Nova Scotia Indians until 1976 when, with assistance from the Secretary of State, it became independent of the Union and came under the guidance of the Native Communications Society, an organization that is not only concerned with the present but maintains extensive files on issues rooted in the eighteenth and nineteenth centuries.

The contributions of the *Micmac News* to Canadian society can be found throughout its pages. It has served as a means whereby the Native people of the Maritimes can express their concerns and opinions, and it had led to an improved self-image among the Micmac through stories dealing with their history, culture and traditions. It has served as a chronicle of events that may be used by Natives and non-Natives alike to appreciate the complexities of life for Micmac living in the Maritimes. Indeed, much of the research upon which parts of this book are based was gleaned from the *Micmac News*. Unfortunately, as this book was being written a federal budget was presented that sought to reduce the national deficit by cutting a multitude of services, including funds towards maintaining the more than twenty Native communications societies across Canada.

The September 1990 issue of the *Micmac News* carried the headline "Micmac News Closes." After more than two decades of serving the Micmac people of the Maritimes, this often controversial paper ended with a special edition highlighting the major issues and events that have confronted the Micmac since the 1960s.

CHAPTER 5
Prominent Individuals

The Micmac people of the Maritimes have contributed greatly to the cultural heritage of eastern Canada. Throughout the history of the region, certain individuals have gained prominence in various fields of endeavour. The author has chosen to highlight mainly those that have contributed to promoting the uniqueness of Micmac culture through literature, the arts and education. This is not meant to downplay the contributions of prominent Micmac to the economic, political or sports heritage of the Maritimes. Further, although individuals are not named, many of today's prominent Micmac provide direction for their people in the important areas discussed in the concluding chapter.

Membertou
The sagamore (chief) Membertou was the first Micmac to be baptized in New France, on June 24, 1610, at Port Royal. However, his exploits and personal character are clouded in the contradictions of history. At the time of the founding of the habitation at Port Royal in 1605, Membertou and his followers were the band most frequently in contact with the emerging French settlement. According to the French explorer Lescarbot, Membertou was more than one hundred years old when the French arrived. In part, this estimate is derived from Membertou's assertion that he had been a mature adult when he met Jacques Cartier, presumably in 1535. His exploits and status among the fifteenth-century Micmac were probably exaggerated both by himself and the French. The French chose to give him pompous titles and names to impress their monarch, Henry IV, including, during the baptismal

ceremonies, the king's first name, Henri. The recognition of Membertou as a great chief was also extended to his family. His wife was named after the queen of France, Marie, and his eldest son was given the name of the dauphin, Louis.

Membertou's own self-image was enhanced by the fact that he was the sagamore in the area that De Monts chose to settle. In effect, Membertou became the host to the Europeans, which meant he was in the most advantageous position to acquire merchandise. This made him the envy of other sagamores whose jealousies earned him a less than credible reputation.

Although a minor sagamore, Membertou's place in the history of the Micmac results from his dealings with the French. He and his band can be attributed with the success of the first attempt at a permanent settlement in New France. Without his alliance the struggling colony could have been easily overrun. Further, his group helped these first Europeans to survive the harsh North American winters. Historical accounts relate that the French abandoned Port Royal from 1607 to 1610, and upon their return the habitation was as they had left it. Here again it was Membertou and his people who had preserved the buildings. The esteem in which the French held this man can be seen in the writings of the Jesuit, Father Pierre Biard, who wrote: "This was the greatest, most renowned and most formidable savage within the memory of man; of splendid physique, taller and larger-limbed than is usual among them; bearded like a Frenchman, although scarcely any of the others have hair upon the chin; grave and reserved; feeling a proper sense of dignity for his position as commander."

Father Biard's notion of the greatness of the sagamore was somewhat shaken when Membertou requested that he be buried with his ancestors. Two days later on his deathbed, on Sunday, September 18, 1611, he changed his mind and requested a resting place among the French. He succumbed to dysentery that day, and his dying wish was honoured on Monday when he was given a solemn Christian funeral.

Mâli Christianne Paul Mollise

Christy Ann Morris, as she was known, was born to the Paul family in 1804, at either Stewiacke or the Ship Harbour Indian reserve. While a young woman she married Tom Mollise, whose family was known to have camped on McNab's Island in Halifax Harbour. The first fifty years of her life are relatively unknown, but after 1850 her history is surprisingly well documented.

In the opinion of Ruth Holmes Whitehead, Mrs. Morris was the finest quillwork artist of her time. Her skills in quillwork and other traditional crafts won her many prizes at provincial exhibitions, including a first prize for a decorated dress in 1845, a first prize for a full-sized birchbark canoe and paddles in 1854, and a first prize for a nest of six quilled boxes in 1868.

The most famous piece of Mrs. Morris's artistic work is housed at the DesBrisay Museum in Bridgewater. In 1868, to commemorate the birth of her friend Reuben Rhuland's son, Christy made a series of quillwork panels to cover a cradle. The work is said to be a copy of one made as a gift for the infant Prince of Wales who later became King Edward VII.

Christy's reputation among the nineteenth-century Haligonian elite as a woman of beauty, virtue and piety led to other forms of recognition. At least seven portraits of her, by various artists, have survived. One of these was done by a talented London artist, Mr. Gush, and presented to the Prince of Wales on his visit to Halifax in 1860.

John J. Sark

John J. Sark is known to be one of the first of the Micmac to receive a college education and was also one of the first to enter into a teaching career in the Maritimes. He was born in Houlton, Maine, in 1888 but lived in the Micmac community of Lennox Island, Prince Edward Island, from early childhood.

After completing his education at Saint Dunstan's College in Charlottetown, he received a third-class provincial teacher's license and assumed a teaching position at the federal Lennox Island school in 1909. According to W. D. Hamilton, John Sark received excellent evaluations for his teaching methods and career as a whole from both school inspectors and Department of Indian Affairs officials.

Unfortunately, John's career was interrupted by local and bureaucratic political controversies over his teaching methods and personal character. Subsequently he was relieved of his teaching duties in 1914 and was replaced by his brother, Jacob, who had also attended Saint Dunstan's College. After serving in the First World War, John Sark once again resumed his teaching position at the Lennox Island school and taught there until his death on April 17, 1945.

During his teaching days, internal and external political animosity continued to hinder the development of education on Lennox Island. In 1938 these controversies split the Lennox Island community. As a result, all but four students were sent to the Shubenacadie Residential School in Nova Scotia. However, slowly, throughout the early winter months, the children began to return, thus saving both the school and John Sark's position.

It should be noted that the 1930s and 1940s were decades of great transition and change for all of the Micmac of the Maritimes. Initially the Shubenacadie school was portrayed as being good for the education of Micmac children. However, all Micmac were to learn that children had to face discrimination, racism and oppression to gain access to this type of non-Micmac education. Also, these were years of centralization, political dictatorship, and confusion for all of the Micmac. Thus, despite the controversies over John Sark's teaching position, he has become a respected historical figure for his leadership and teaching skills, and for showing both Micmac and non-Micmac alike that his people could assume the responsibility of educating their own children. It is evident that John Sark passed his qualities on to his children—one of his sons, Jack Sark, is the current chief of Lennox Island. John Sark is still remembered and honoured by the Micmac of Lennox Island and in the rest of the Maritimes. The John J. Sark Memorial School on Lennox Island was dedicated in 1981 and is an example of one way in which the memory of this man will be passed on to future generations.

Marie Battiste

Marie Battiste received her Doctor of Education degree at Stanford University in California in 1984 and is recognized as the first Micmac to achieve such a high academic standard.

Although her roots are in the Eskasoni community, Marie was born in Houlton, Maine. Discouraged by the centralization process of the 1940s, and feeling the impact of racism and prejudice suffered by Marie's older sister at the Shubenacadie Residential School, Marie's father felt that the United States offered better educational and employment opportunities.

While growing up in Maine, Marie and her family stayed in contact

Dr. Marie Battiste receives an honorary Doctor of Letters from Saint Mary's University.

Prominent Individuals 51

and frequently visited family and friends at the Eskasoni and Chapel Island reserves in Nova Scotia. As a result, Marie always knew her Micmac roots and she also learned and spoke the Micmac language in her own home. Aware of the general lack of knowledge and appreciation of early Micmac history, language, culture, and the resulting loss of identity, Marie dedicated her efforts to the education of Native peoples.

After receiving her Bachelor of Science degree at the University of Maine in 1971, Marie taught at a Passamaquoddy and a Penobscot reserve in Maine. Shortly thereafter, she was encouraged to remain at the University of Maine to help launch a program for disadvantaged youth. Two years later, with the encouragement of a Passamaquoddy friend, Marie applied and was accepted into a master's program in Education and Administration at Harvard University. After completing her master's degree in 1974, Marie was recruited by the State of Maine as a director for early childhood education programs for "Indian" reserves. These programs are still in operation today.

Marie later taught "Indian" education at the University of California where her husband also worked, and at the same time she started her doctorate program at Stanford University. She temporarily discontinued this program and took a position with the Union of Nova Scotia Indians to do research on the Micmac language in the Eskasoni community.

After taking time off to be with her newborn son, Marie continued with her doctorate research, which was focused on the social and historical background of Micmac writing systems. She later declined an offer to teach at Trent University to take the combined position of director of education and principal at the Mi'kmawey School for the Chapel Island Indian Band. She helped build a Micmac-based curriculum that included the Micmac language. Marie Battiste is now a full-time cultural curriculum development coordinator for the Eskasoni school system.

Marie is well known for her academic and public achievements. In 1975 she was awarded the American Indian Program Fellowship and in 1985 was named the Women of the Year by the Professional Women's Business Society. In 1986 she received the Alumni Achievement Award from the University of Maine, and in 1987 she received an honorary Doctor of Letters degree from Saint Mary's University in Halifax. Marie has also had several articles published on Micmac literacy and education.

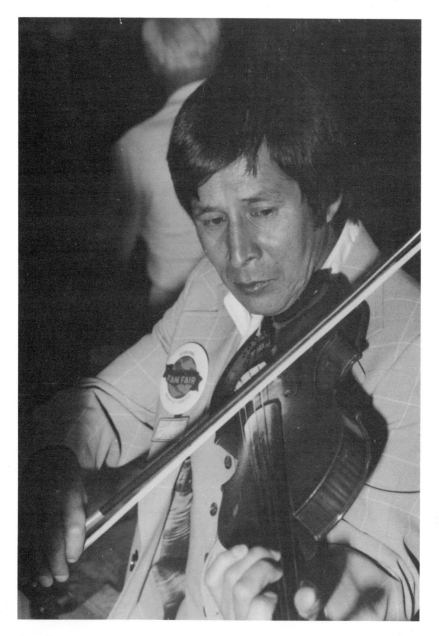

Lee Cremo.

Micmac News

Prominent Individuals   53

With such dedication and high achievements, Marie Battiste has become a well respected and honoured leader in Micmac education throughout the Micmac nation and North America. Her contributions to Micmac education are invaluable and will always be remembered by the Micmac of the Maritimes.

Lee Cremo

Lee Cremo, a Micmac fiddler, is a well known and highly respected musician. He was born on the Chapel Island reserve on Cape Breton Island in 1938. At the age of five, Lee and his family moved to Eskasoni as a result of the centralization process. During his early childhood, he was introduced to fiddle music by his father, Simon, who was well known for his musical talents. When Lee was eight, his father was seriously ill, and Lee decided that it was important to pick up where his dad had left off.

For many years he played the fiddle in the privacy of his home, but in 1965, with the encouragement and support of his friend Charlie Gould, he played at the Maritime Fiddling Championship at Halifax. Although he did not know all of the rules and subsequently was not very successful, this did not discourage him. He played at the championship the following year and won, and kept on winning until 1968. After three consecutive wins, the regulations required him to step aside. Entering again in 1970, Lee Cremo won the championship for another three consecutive years.

He has played in several bands and now plays solo. Lee has not only brought music to many Micmac gatherings and special occasions, but also to national events such as Expo '67 in Montreal and the Commonwealth games in Edmonton. Lee has appeared in two films: "The Vanishing Cape Breton Fiddle," produced by CBC and aired in 1971, and "Arms of Gold," produced by Whippett & Edwin Communications in 1985.

Lee Cremo strongly encourages all Micmac youth to take up their musical aspirations, and he hopes that those interested in the fiddle will carry on the tradition of Micmac fiddle music in the Maritimes.

Rita Joe

Rita Joe, a well known Micmac poet of the Maritimes, has become

Rita Joe.

Micmac News

a prominent and greatly respected writer across Canada and abroad. Her first two books, the *Poems of Rita Joe* and *Song of Eskasoni*, have brought pride to her people and an understanding and respect of the Micmac experience to the general public.

Rita was born on the Whycocomagh reserve in 1932. Following her mother's death, Rita, at the age of five, lived in several "Indian" foster homes throughout Nova Scotia. At the age of twelve, Rita decided to take her destiny into her own hands by writing a letter to the Indian agent at the Indianbrook reserve, requesting that she be placed in the Shubenacadie Residential School. Her request was granted and she stayed at the school for four years. Rita held several jobs in Halifax, Montreal and Boston, including working at an orphanage. She met her husband (now deceased) in Boston during the 1950s and now lives in the Eskasoni community and is a mother of ten, including two foster children.

It was the negative and racist portrayal of the Micmac in her children's history books that inspired Rita to write. She felt that it was important to pass on a sense of Micmac pride and dignity to her children and all of the Micmac nation, and thus Rita dedicated her writings to demonstrating the little known and positive side of the Micmac way of life.

Writing since 1969, Rita's poems were continually published in the *Micmac News*. In 1974 she submitted a collection of her works entitled "Valiant Race" to a literary competition sponsored by the Nova Scotia Writers Federation. Placing third, Rita proudly accepted her prize dressed in Micmac costume at the awards ceremony.

In 1979 Rita accepted an invitation by the Abenaki Press to publish her poetry. Ten years later, Rita launched her second book, published by Ragweed Press of Prince Edward Island.

Rita Joe continues to represent the Micmac of the Maritimes as a guest speaker and lecturer at educational institutions and public gatherings throughout North America. Her third book is intended for the Grade 3 to 6 audience in the public school system. Rita is also working on projects that address contemporary Micmac issues, from social injustice to Native rights.

Rita believes in education as a mechanism for eliminating the preconceptions of the Micmac in the non-Native society and for transforming a Micmac sense of defeatism into a sense of positive pride, dignity and self-respect. She encourages all youth to obtain an education and to write about their own experiences.

As a preserver of Micmac culture and an advocate of the elimination of racism and discrimination, Rita Joe has become a well known writer and leader and will continue to be an honoured and respected member of Micmac society for generations to come.

Joseph M. Augustine.

Joseph M. Augustine

Joseph Augustine was born on March 16, 1911, at Bid Cove, New Brunswick. As a young boy he and his family moved to Red Bank, where he was later to become a prominent member of the community. He married Mary Metallic from the Restigouche reserve and they settled at Red Bank to raise their family of eight children. Joe provided for his family by fishing, hunting, trapping, logging and guiding on the Miramichi. He supplemented his income by manufacturing ash baskets, a craft of which he is a noted master.

Joe's commitment to Red Bank resulted in his being elected as chief for two terms (1952-54 and 1956-58); he also served as a Band councillor for two terms (1960-64 and 1966-72). During these terms in office he continued to pursue a traditional way of life. In 1987 he was awarded the Certificate of Excellence from the Hudson Bay Company for the highest quality pelts submitted in Canada.

Throughout his life, Joe Augustine maintained a close relationship with the natural world found along the Miramichi River system. His familiarity with the region and his memory of his father showing him a "special place" thought to have been used in the past for ceremonial dancing, led Joe to discover one of the most spectacular archaeological sites in the Maritimes.

In 1972 Joe explored a low earthen mound located between the Northwest Miramichi and Little Southwest Miramichi rivers. There he encountered a burial place of his ancestors. His persistence and determination led to an excavation being undertaken by the New Brunswick Department of Tourism, Recreation and Heritage in 1975. The team was directed by Dr. Christopher Turnbull and included Joe, his daughter Madeline and his son Howard.

The burial site is now known as the Augustine Mound. The human remains and artifacts date back to more than 2,400 years ago. It is one of the most easterly mounds related to the Adena burial tradition, which was centred in the Ohio River valley. The site contained human remains, as well as various ornaments, stone pipes, clay vessels, copper and shell beads, and preserved woven fabrics.

Joe also discovered the Oxbow site, a habitation site located approximately one kilometre west of the mound, that represents a continuously occupied fishing site dating to 500 B.C.

The importance of Joe's discoveries led to both being designated as national historic sites. In 1984, as a bicentennial project, the Province of New Brunswick commissioned a film on Red Bank entitled *Metepengiag: A Village through Time* which portrays the history of the community over 3,000 years. It relates the way of life of the Micmac people of Red Bank as they occupied the Oxbow site and buried their dead at the Augustine Mound. The movie appears in English and Micmac, with the latter having been translated by Mildred Milliea of Big Cove.

In 1988, Joe Augustine received the provincial Minister's Award for Heritage "in recognition of his contribution to the history of the Micmac people and the heritage of the Province of New Brunswick."

CHAPTER 6

Micmac in the Maritimes in the 1980s and 1990s

I. New Directions

About 70 percent of the approximately 14,000 Micmac in the Maritimes are found on twenty-five major reserves, of which three are on Prince Edward Island, nine in New Brunswick and thirteen in Nova Scotia. The total number of reserves in the Maritimes is actually greater, but these twenty-five are those that have substantial numbers of Micmac living on them. The vacant reserves came into being in the 1940s when the Department of Indian Affairs carried out a centralization program that moved many people living on the dozens of small reserves into larger settlements. The Micmac had been encouraged to make the move by promises of new homes and better educational and economic opportunities. However, these promises proved to be shallow because the only employment to be found was in the construction of their new homes and in a few public works programs.

Although the resettlement of people onto the larger reserves had many problems, it inadvertently allowed for the growth of political structures on these reserves. The revised Indian Act of 1951 gave broader powers to Band councils over community affairs, in an early attempt to prepare various reserves for "self-determination." The Micmac of the time were suspicious of this policy, fearing it was an attempt by the federal government to transfer the responsibility for Native peoples' rights to the various provincial administrations.

The 1960s brought many changes in the political, economic and educational opportunities afforded the Micmac. These changes resulted in part from a general trend throughout the rural areas and small towns of the Maritimes. Increased interest and government funds for the health and welfare of all Maritimers led to improvements in basic services on reserves such as electricity, sewers and highways. The late 1960s and early 1970s were a time when world events influenced many people, particularly youth. The movement across North America towards pan-Indianism made young Micmac and adult leaders aware of problems and programs among Native peoples in Canada and the United States.

The late 1960s saw national and regional organizations forming alliances to combat common problems and to confront various issues related to land claims, inadequate education, and loss of ethnic identity. It was during this time that the Bands within the provinces joined to present a united front. Thus the Union of Nova Scotia Indians and the Union of New Brunswick Indians both came into being. Communication among Band members and Micmac living off the reserves was facilitated by the publication of the monthly newspaper, *Micmac News*. The creation of the unions provided opportunities for collective lobbying efforts, workshops, conferences and policy statements.

The unionized approach to common issues, the search for ethnic identity, and the movement towards "self-determination" accelerated in the 1980s. To some this growth in creating organizations was seen as creating factions among the people. There is some truth in this, but the splits have deep historical roots and some divisions were dictated by the needs of local or regional Bands with specific problems. Other divisions reflect political reality, in that the Micmac of Nova Scotia must deal with their provincial government as must those in New Brunswick and Prince Edward Island.

Perhaps the most important political event for all Canadians in the 1980s was the repatriation of the Canadian Constitution. Within that document are several provisions related to aboriginal people, including Section 35, which recognized and affirmed aboriginal and treaty rights. Unfortunately, the interpretation of treaties remains a legal issue with two sides, and thus the aboriginal rights protected in many early treaties are now subject to interpretation by the courts. One example is the Micmac right to manage their own hunting activities which, though guaranteed in treaties, is all under the purview of provincial legislation.

The recognition of former treaty rights became a dominant issue in the 1980s. In particular, the Treaty or Articles of Peace and Friendship Renewed that ended the hostilities between the Micmac and the British in 1752 was cited in many court appearances. To many, this treaty unequivocally guaranteed Micmac hunting and fishing rights in perpetuity. The article stating this reads: "It is agreed that the said Tribe of Indians [the Micmac] shall not be hindered from, but have free liberty of hunting and fishing as usual and . . . the Indians shall have liberty . . . to sell, where they shall . . . dispose thereof to the best Advantage." Although the Supreme Court of Canada upheld this treaty in 1985, the government of Nova Scotia challenged this decision.

The Micmac accepted that challenge and launched cases to assert their traditional moose-hunting rights. Further they used the Supreme Court ruling to initiate a more comprehensive breach of trust suit. Through their actions in and out of court, Micmac demonstrated their dissatisfaction with the status quo.

A second part of the Constitution, Section 25, provided that the guarantees contained in the Canadian Charter of Rights and Freedoms would not be interpreted so as to abrogate or derogate from aboriginal, treaty, or other rights or freedoms. This section led to one of the first major changes in Canada's Indian Act since 1876, when in June 1985 the Canadian Parliament passed Bill C-31, an Act to Amend the Indian Act. The amendment was guided by three principles: the elimination of discrimination, the restoration of status and membership rights, and the increase of Natives' control over their own affairs. The discrimination clause focused mainly on status registration, which previously contained sexually discriminatory criteria. Bill C-31 removed the procedure whereby a Micmac woman who married a non-Micmac lost her status. Further it permitted women and men who had lost their status through discrimination or enfranchisement to have it restored.

II. Micmac Self-Government

Before Europeans colonized the Maritimes, the Micmac peoples possessed a form of government. The sagamores, or chiefs, had territories which they effectively controlled. Their leadership was at the will of the people and depended upon their personal qualities and abilities to provide for their people. Contact with the French and English regimes reduced much of the authority held by various sagamores. Their authority was further reduced by the proclamation of the Indian lands legislation in 1868 and the Indian Act in 1876. The basic right of the Micmac to control their own destiny was eroded further under various Indian Affairs administrations.

Although the injustices have gradually eased in recent decades, the

Micmac have yet to gain full responsibility for their own government. Today, in their view, aboriginal self-government is necessary for the achievement of the changes they desire, such as jurisdiction over land, resources, social services, child welfare, and economic development.

The dominance of "the two founding peoples" (the French and English) in Canada has directed the affairs of the country from its beginning. It was only recognized in recent decades that Canada is a multicultural nation. The 1971 royal commission report, which led Prime Minister Trudeau to declare the "Just Society," sought to guarantee social equality and freedom of choice for all of Canada's ethnic minorities. Although, on the surface, a multicultural ideology would seem to allow for the recognition of distinct societies within the mosaic of Canadian culture, the pervasive policy for Native peoples remains one of assimilation. This is particularly true in the area of education.

III. Education

Federal government policies on "Indian education" have always reflected assimilation initiatives rather than the educational needs identified by the Native peoples themselves. Since the assimilationist policies of the 1960s, aboriginal nations across Canada have been seeking to control their own educational programs.

As a result of national aboriginal lobbying efforts, the federal government adopted a policy of "Indian control of Indian education" in 1973. However, Native peoples are still finding that their control is influenced and restricted by policies set forth by the federal government,

In 1989, another policy on "Indian" post-secondary education was imposed without consultation with Native peoples. This policy not only included many cutbacks on student financial assistance but represented another attempt to dictate Indian self-government. Micmac post-secondary students, education directors, counsellors, and Band governments have been organizing themselves, locally, provincially, regionally and nationally in order to control and set their own educational objectives.

Micmac of the Maritimes are working to establish a community-based consultation process to identify Micmac educational needs. This is part of a national objective, through the National Indian Brotherhood and Assembly of First Nations organizations, to establish a system of consultation and educational programs from the local to national levels.

At the regional level, Micmac education directors and counsellors have met regularly to discuss policies on Native education and to exchange information on their different programs. These meetings are organized and paid for by the Micmac and are independent of the Department of Indian Affairs. Out of these meetings, the Micmac have discovered that the Department of Indian Affairs has not been consistent in providing funding for similar programs throughout the Maritimes. Thus, this consultation process has provided a forum where the Micmac of the Maritimes can address these issues collectively and discourage future political inconsistency.

The biggest challenge facing the Micmac of the Maritimes and aboriginal nations across Canada is obtaining federal and provincial recognition of Native education as an aboriginal right. However, the work of the Micmac has already helped to create an awareness of these issues within other educational institutions in the Maritimes.

Some Micmac have been invited to give inservice training to teachers in the Maritimes. Many Micmac organizations are now in the process of writing their own history and developing educational tools such as films and other materials. Significant progress has also been made in developing educational programs in post-secondary institutions. In the early 1970s, St. Thomas University in Fredericton, New Brunswick, established the first Native Studies Program, which was later followed by the Micmac-Maliseet Institute. Although the Micmac-Maliseet Institute did not receive its official title until 1981, its activities began in the mid-1970s and it has become recognized for its development programs in education for Micmac and Maliseet teachers and students, and for its community leadership programs.

More recently, a Dalhousie Law program was established for indigenous Blacks and Micmac. The minority students are required to take the same courses and pass the same examinations as other law students, but different admission requirements are applied to the minority students. They are admitted on the basis of their academic record, entrance exams and other factors, including community involvement and employment experiences. The program is funded by an annual grant from the Nova Scotia Law Foundation, and a portion of this grant is used to hire senior students as tutors to help the minority students.

Inroads have also been made in the health and science fields in education for both community workers and Micmac students interested in related careers.

The Micmac Friendship Centre in Halifax has played a significant role in assisting the Micmac with educational upgrading and university preparation skills, as has the Transition Year Program at Dalhousie University.

These directions in education will provide the basis for the Micmac in the Maritimes to determine their own needs and objectives, and will be invaluable to the development of Micmac self-government and self-determination.

IV. Health

Health issues are a priority concern for the Micmac of the Maritimes. Many Bands, organizations and tribal councils are in the process of assuming control over a variety of programs that were previously under the exclusive jurisdiction of the Department of Indian Affairs and the Medical Services Branch of Health and Welfare Canada. These include the community health representative programs, dental and medical consultant programs and Native alcohol and drug abuse counselling and prevention programs.

Intensive research and studies are continuing that allow the Micmac to assess their own health needs and to design their own health plans at the community level. Significant progress has also been made on the initiation of Micmac health education and related careers. By 1989, most of the community health representatives were Micmac and there were twelve to fifteen registered nurses throughout the Maritimes.

Micmac efforts at self-determination led to the founding of the Micmac Children and Family Services Program in Nova Scotia in the mid-1980s. Under this program the Micmac can now legally assume responsibility for and determine the destiny of their own children.

Tremendous progress has been made in the area of alcohol and drug abuse rehabilitation programs. These include the Mi-Kmaw Lodge at Eskasoni and the Eagle's Nest at Indianbrook, both founded by the executive director of the Nova Scotia Native Alcohol and Drug Counselling Program, Joseph H. Denny. Mr. Denny has been involved in this program for several years and is well known for his dedication and commitment to encouraging prevention, and creating rehabilitation programs for the Eel River, Big Cove, Tobique, and Kings Clear communities of New Brunswick.

Despite the many difficulties and obstacles yet to be overcome for full Micmac self-government and self-determination, these developments in Micmac health have opened the door for future generations.

V. Justice

One of the major issues facing the Micmac during the 1980s was the unequal treatment of Natives and other people by the Maritime justice systems. This issue was brought to a head by the wrongful conviction of Donald Marshall Jr. The tragedy began in a park in Sydney in 1971 where a young man was murdered. Mr. Marshall was accused of this crime and served eleven years in prison for a murder he did not commit. An exhaustive enquiry has exonerated him of all blame with the summary notation that his wrongful conviction came about "in part at least [because] Donald Marshall Jr. is a Native."

The initial miscarriage of justice resulted from prejudice and "dereliction of duty" on the part of the investigating agencies. A 1989 royal commission report notes that the criminal justice system of 1971 was woefully inadequate because it was dominated by white males whose verdicts were sometimes influenced in various ways. The court that acquitted Donald Marshall Jr. in 1983 was still not prepared to take the opportunity to stimulate improvement of a system that wrongfully placed a seventeen year old in prison; rather, this court defended the system at Donald Marshall's expense. The appeals court found that "Marshall was the author of his own misfortune." In making this statement they accused Marshall of lies he did not tell and convicted him of a robbery which he did not commit and for which he was not even charged. The onus for determining his own innocence was placed squarely on the shoulders of Marshall himself. Fortunately for all Canadians, this travesty of justice was not allowed to stand unanswered.

In 1986 the Province of Nova Scotia established a royal commission on the Donald Marshall Jr. case. Four years later the commission released its report in seven volumes containing eighty-two recommendations. The purpose of the recommendations is to improve the justice system of Nova Scotia. However, when the commission was established, its powers were limited to recommendations only, which may or may not be accepted by the government. It is interesting to note that many of the recommendations deal with visible minorities in the criminal justice system and pay particular attention to the plight of Natives and Blacks. However, as with many royal commission reports, it remains the responsibility of the people of Canada to ensure that their elected representatives act in a responsible manner.

The Micmac struggle for the right to self-determination extends into many facets of Native life, including justice. A number of the recommendations in the royal commission's report address this issue as it applied to legal initiatives. One major recommendation is to establish a community-controlled Native criminal court. A suggested five-year pilot project would include a number of elements such as a Native justice of the peace who would hear cases involving summary conviction offences that occur on a reserve. Depending upon the nature of the offence, the local community would have a means to make recommendations for sentencing, including the possibility of community work projects on a reserve as an alternative to fines and/or imprisonment. In those cases where imprisonment is deemed necessary, mechanisms are needed on the reserves for probation and aftercare.

Many of the recommendations of the Marshall royal commission centre on education for both Native peoples and members of police forces and the judiciary. It is sad that our modern society needs to be reminded that systematic discrimination still plays a role in the justice system. A public inquiry should not have to recommend that "factors which are to be excluded from consideration in determining whether the public interest requires a prosecution include: the alleged offender's race, religion, sex, national origin, political associations, or beliefs," The pain and anguish experienced by Donald Marshall Jr., a victim of racial discrimination, should not go unheeded by Maritimers, no matter what their ethnic origin.

VI. Looking Forward

The Micmac of the 1990s will face many challenges to their culture, and their long struggle to maintain their distinctive character in the cultural mosaic of Canadian society will continue. However, they have a determination to succeed and will no doubt enter the next century as a proud and respected people.

APPENDIX 1
1752 Treaty

ENCLOSURE IN LETTER OF GOVERNOR HOPSON TO THE RIGHT HONOURABLE THE EARL OF HOLDERNESSE 6TH OF DEC. 1752 TREATY OR ARTICLES OF PEACE AND FRIENDSHIP RENEWED

Between

His Excellency Pereprine Thomas Hopson Esquire Captain General and Governor in Chief in and over His Majesty's Province of Nova Scotia or Acadie Vice Admiral of the same and Colonal of One of His Majesty's Regiments of Foot, and His Majesty's Council on behalf of His Majesty.

And

Major Jean Baptiste Cope chief Sacham of the Tribe of Mick Mack Indians, inhabiting the Eastern Coast of the said Province, and Andrew Hadley Martin, Gabriel Martin and Francis Jeremiah members & Delegates of the said Tribe, for themselves and their said Tribe their heirs and the heirs of their heirs forever. Begun made and Concluded in the manner form & Tenor following, viz.

1. It is agreed that the Articles of Submission & Agreements made at Boston in New England by the Delegates of the Penobscot Norridgwolk & St. John's Indians in the Year 1725 Ratifyed and Confirmed by all the Nova Scotia Tribes at Annapolis Royal in the Month of June 1726 and lately Renewed with Governor Cornwallis at Halifax and Ratifyed at St. John's River, now read over Explained & Interpreted shall be and are hereby from this time forward renewed, reiterated and forever Confirmed by them and their Tribe, and the said Indians for themselves and their Tribe, and their Heirs aforesaid do make and renew the same Solemn Submissions and promises for the strict Observance of all the Articles therein Contained as at any time heretofore hath been done.

2. That all Transactions during the late War shall on both sides be buried in Oblivion with the Hatchet, And that the said Indians shall have all

favour, Friendship & Protection shewn them from this His Majesty's Government.

3. That the said Tribe shall use their utmost Endeavours to bring in the other Indians to Renew and Ratify this Peace, and shall discover and make known any attempts or designs of any other Indians or any Enemy whatever against his Majesty's Subjects within this Province so soon as they shall know thereof and shall also hinder and Obstruct the same to the utmost of their power, and on the other hand if any of the Indians refusing to ratify this Peace shall make War upon the Tribe who have now Confirmed the same; they shall upon Application have such aid and Assistance from the Government for their defence as the Case may require.

4. It is agreed that the said Tribe of Indians shall not be hindered from, but have free liberty of hunting and Fishing as usual and that if they shall think a Truck house needful at the River Chibenaccadie, or any other place of their resort they shall have the same built and proper Merchandize, lodged therein to be exchanged for what the Indians shall have to dispose of and that in the mean time the Indians shall have free liberty to bring to Sale to Halifax or any other settlement within this province, Skins, feathers, fowl, fish or any other thing they shall have to sell, where they shall have liberty to dispose thereof to the best Advantage.

5. That a Quality of bread, flour, and such other Provisions, as be procured, necessary for the Familys and proportionable to the Numbers of the said Indians, shall be given them half Yearly for the time to come; and the same regard shall be bad to the other Tribes that shall thereafter Agree to Renew and Ratify the Peace upon the Terms and Conditions now Stipulated.

6. That to Cherish a good harmony and mutual Correspondence between the said Indians and this Government His Excellency Peregrine Thomas Hopson Esq. Capt. General & Governor in Chief in & over His Majesty's Province of Nova Scotia or Acadie Vice Admiral of the same & Colonel of One of His Majesty's Regiments of Foot hereby promises on the part of His Majesty that the said Indians shall upon the First Day of October Yearly, so long as they shall Continue in Friendship, Receive Presents of Blankets, Tobacco, some Powder & Shot, and the said Indians promise once every year, upon the first of October, to come by themselves or their

Delegates and Receive the said Presents and Renew their Friendship and Submissions.

7. That the Indians shall use their best Endeavors to save the Lives & Goods of any People Shipwrecked on this Coast where they resort and shall Conduct the People saved to Halifax with their Goods, and a Reward adequate to the Salvage shall be given them.

8. That all Disputes whatsoever that may happen to arise between the Indians now at Peace and others His Majesty's Subjects in this Province shall be tryed in His Majesty's Courts of Civil Judicature, where the Indians shall have the same benefits, Advantages & Priviledges as any others of His Majesty's Subjects.

In Faith & Testimony whereof the Great Seal of the Province is hereunto appended, and the Partys to these Presents have hereunto interchangeably Set their Hands in the Council Chamber at Halifax this 22nd day of Nov. 1752 in the 26th Year of His Majesty's Reign.

P. T. Hopson	Jean Baptiste Cope	X	His Mark
Chas. Lawrence	Andrew Hadley	X	
Benj. Green	Francois	X	
Jno. Salusbury	Gabriel	X	
Willm. Steele			
Jno. Collier			

Micmac Reserves

NOVA SCOTIA

Reserve	Reserve No.	Band	Approx. Acres
Sydney	28A & B	Sydney	81
Caribou Marsh	29	Sydney	536
Eskasoni	3	Eskasoni	8,660
Eskasoni	3A	Eskasoni	68
Margaree	25	Middle River	2
Middle River	1	Middle River	773
Chapel Island	5	Chapel Island	1,273
Malagawatch	4	All Cape Breton Bands	1,200
Whycocomagh	2	Whycocomagh	1,528
Port Hood	26	Whycocomagh	(?)
Pomquet & Afton	23	Afton	519
Merigomish Harbour	31	Pictou Landing	35
Boat Harbour West	37	Pictou Landing	200
Fishers Grant	24, 24G	Pictou Landing	383
Sheet Harbour	36	Truro	77
Beaver Lake	17	Truro	100
Truro	27A, B & C	Truro	120
Millbrook	27	Truro	761
Shubenacadie	14	Shubenacadie	2,998
Shubenacadie	13	Shubenacadie	1,018
Cole Harbour	30	Truro	44
St. Croix	34	Annapolis Valley	263
Horton	35	Annapolis Valley	423
New Ross	20	Shubenacadie	1,000

Pennal	19	Shubenacadie	100
Cambridge	32	Annapolis Valley	47
Cold River	21	Acadia	900
Wildcat	12	Acadia	1,150
Medway River	11	Acadia	10
Ponhook Lake	10	Acadia	200
Bear River	6A	Bear River	76
Bear River	6	Bear River	1,594
Yarmouth	33	Acadia	21
Franklin Manor	22	Afton & Pictou Landing	1,000

PRINCE EDWARD ISLAND

Lennox Island	1	Lennox Island	2,415
Rocky Point	3	Lennox Island	3
Scotch Fort	4	Lennox Island	140
Morell	2	Lennox Island	183

NEW BRUNSWICK

The Brothers	18	All N.B. Micmac	10
Buctouche	16	Buctouche	352
Pokemouche	13	Burnt Church	485
Tabusintac	9	Burnt Church	8,077
Burnt Church	14	Burnt Church	2,052
Indian Island	28	Indian Island	100
Richibucto	15	Big Cove	2,609
Eel Ground	2	Eel Ground	2,682
Indian Point	1	Red Bank	100
Renous	12	Eel Ground	25
Red Bank	4	Red Bank	3,773
Red Bank	7	Red Bank	2,353
Big Hole Tract	8	Eel Ground & Red Bank	5,846
Eel River	3	Eel River	442
Papineau	11	Papineau	982

Source: Department of Indian and Northern Development, *Atlas of Indian Reserves and Settlements of Canada 1971*, Ottawa.

Bibliography

MacDonald, George F. *Debert: A Paleo-Indian Site in Central Nova Scotia.* National Museum of Man, Anthropology Papers 16. Ottawa, 1968.

Reid, John G. *Six Crucial Decades: Times of Change in the History of the Maritimes.* Halifax: Nimbus, 1987.

Sanger, David. *Cow Point: An Archaic Cemetery in New Brunswick.* National Museum of Man, Archaeological Survey of Canada, Mercury Series 12. Ottawa, 1973.

Sanger, David. *The Carson Site and the Late Ceramic Period in Passamaquoddy Bay, New Brunswick.* National Museum of Man, Archaeological Survey of Canada, Mercury Series 135. Ottawa, 1987.

Sheldon, Helen L. *The Late Prehistory of Nova Scotia as Viewed from the Brown Site.* Nova Scotia Museum, Curatorial Report 61. Halifax, 1988.

Tuck, James A. *Ancient People of Port au Choix: The Excavation of an Archaic Indian Cemetery in Newfoundland.* Newfoundland Social and Economic Studies 17. St. John's, 1976.

Tuck, James A. *Maritime Provinces Prehistory.* National Museum of Man. Ottawa, 1984.

Upton, L. F. S. *Micmac and Colonists: Indian-White Relations in the Maritimes, 1713-1867.* Vancouver: University of British Columbia Press, 1979.

Wallis, W. D., & R. S. Wallis. *The Micmac Indians of Eastern Canada*. Minneapolis: University of Minnesota Press, 1955.

Whitehead, Ruth Holmes. *Micmac Quillwork.*. Halifax: Nova Scotia Museum, 1983.

Whitehead, Ruth Holmes, & Harold McGee. *The Micmac*. Halifax: Nimbus, 1983.